YOUR PASSPORT TO

FRANCE

by Charly Haley

CONTENT CONSULTANT

Céline Brossillon, PhD
Assistant Professor of Modern Languages
Ursinus College

CAPSTONE PRESS
a capstone imprint

Capstone Captivate is published by Capstone Press, an imprint of Capstone.
1710 Roe Crest Drive
North Mankato, Minnesota 56003
www.capstonepub.com

Library of Congress Cataloging-in-Publication Data
Names: Haley, Charly, author.
Title: Your passport to France / by Charly Haley.
Description: North Mankato, Minnesota : Capstone Press, [2021] | Series: World passport | Includes index. | Audience: Grades 4-6.
Identifiers: LCCN 2020001096 (print) | LCCN 2020001097 (ebook) | ISBN 9781496684059 (hardcover) | ISBN 9781496687975 (paperback) | ISBN 9781496684561 (pdf)
Subjects: LCSH: France--Juvenile literature.
Classification: LCC DC17 .H25 2021 (print) | LCC DC17 (ebook) | DDC 944--dc23
LC record available at https://lccn.loc.gov/2020001096
LC ebook record available at https://lccn.loc.gov/2020001097

Image Credits
iStockphoto: Gregory_DUBUS, 23, serts, 24; Red Line Editorial: 5; Shutterstock Images: Anatoly Tiplyashin, cover (flag), Catarina Belova, cover (bottom), Everett - Art, 9, FrimuFilms, 14, Hung Chung Chih, 6, kan_khampanya, 13, Leonard Zhukovsky, 28, Natashadub, cover (map), Radu Razvan, 27, s4svisuals, 19, Stefano Ember, 20, Takashi Images, 16
Design Elements: iStockphoto, Shutterstock Images

Editorial Credits
Editor: Jamie Hudalla; Designer: Colleen McLaren

Printed in the United States of America.
PA117

CONTENTS

Words in **bold** are in the glossary.

CHAPTER ONE

WELCOME TO FRANCE!

The Eiffel Tower shines over the city of Paris, France. This tall metal tower lights up at night. People think it looks beautiful. More than 7 million people visit it each year.

The Eiffel Tower is one of many famous places in France. France is a country in western Europe. More than 65 million people live there. Most of them speak French. Some speak English too. France has many **immigrants** from north Africa. They often speak a language called Arabic.

People from all over the world love to visit France. The country has many **monuments** and museums that show its rich history. Many of these places are in Paris, which is the country's capital city. People also visit France's beaches, mountains, and countryside.

MAP OF FRANCE

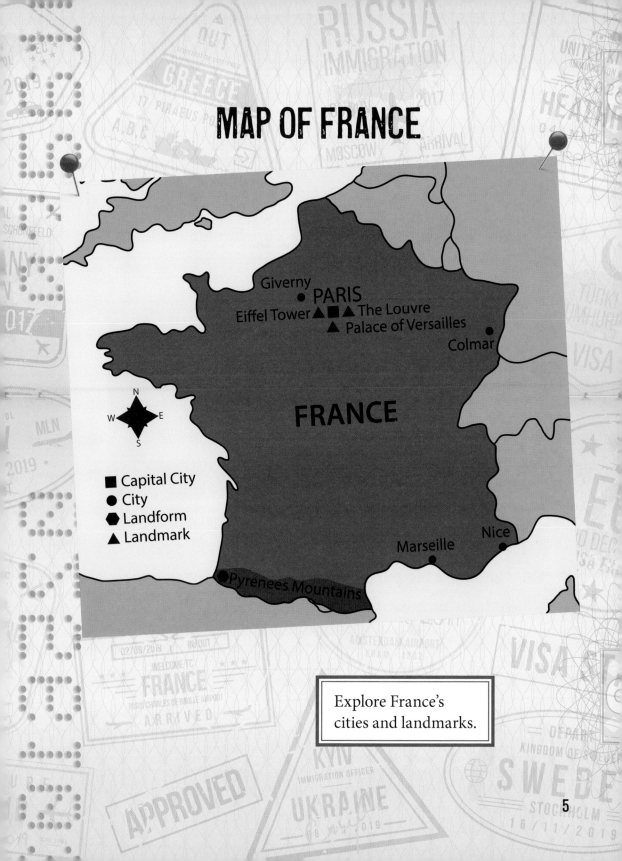

Giverny
● PARIS
Eiffel Tower ▲■▲ The Louvre
▲ Palace of Versailles
● Colmar

FRANCE

N
W ✦ E
S

■ Capital City
● City
⬡ Landform
▲ Landmark

Marseille
Nice

● Pyrenees Mountains

Explore France's cities and landmarks.

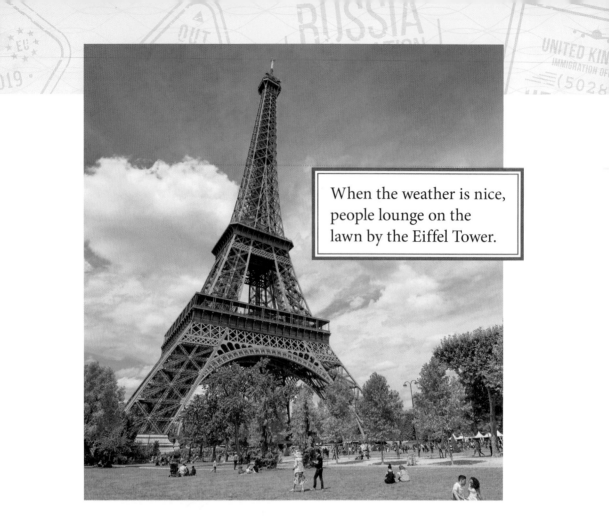

When the weather is nice, people lounge on the lawn by the Eiffel Tower.

FRENCH CULTURE

Food is a big part of French **culture**. French people take their time eating meals and shopping for fresh ingredients. Many people go to outdoor markets for fresh foods such as fruits and vegetables. Some vendors sell their food every day, while other markets might occur once a week.

FACT FILE

OFFICIAL NAME: .... FRENCH REPUBLIC
POPULATION: 65,097,000
LAND AREA: .... 210,026 SQ. MI. (543,965 SQ KM)
CAPITAL: .... PARIS
MONEY: .... EURO
GOVERNMENT: .... ELECTED PRESIDENT
LANGUAGE: .... FRENCH

GEOGRAPHY: Located in western Europe, France borders Spain, Belgium, Luxembourg, Germany, Switzerland, and Italy. It also borders the Atlantic Ocean, the Mediterranean Sea, and the English Channel. Most of the north and west parts of the country are flat. Southern France has mountains, including the Alps and Pyrenees. France has islands, such as Corsica, off its coasts.

NATURAL RESOURCES: France is among the countries that make the most wind energy. This means it uses wind to make electricity. France also has a lot of coal mines in the north.

France is known for its art, fashion, and more. The country hosts the famous Tour de France bicycle race. Many French people show their pride by sharing their history and culture in their various museums.

CHAPTER TWO

HISTORY OF FRANCE

In the 770s, King Charlemagne ruled over the area that is now France. He took control over other parts of western Europe too. He wanted people to come together and practice Christianity. Early French kings made this religion a big part of their **governing**.

THE FRENCH REVOLUTION

Louis XVI and Marie Antoinette were among the last kings and queens of France. Their rule ended in 1792 after French citizens took over the government.

JOAN OF ARC

France was in a war for 116 years in the 1300s and 1400s called the Hundred Years War. An 18-year-old woman named Joan of Arc led a part of the French army. She helped win a major battle in 1429. Joan of Arc became famous across France. But a year later, an English leader of the Catholic church said she was a witch and had her killed. Today Joan of Arc is a beloved figure of France.

Marie Antoinette was famous for her fashion.

TIMELINE OF FRENCH HISTORY

768–814: King Charlemagne rules the area that is now France.

1429: Joan of Arc leads a French army to victory during the Hundred Years War.

1643–1715: King Louis XIV rules France.

1774–1792: King Louis XVI and Marie Antoinette are king and queen of France.

1787–1799: People fight to overthrow the monarchy during the French Revolution.

1804–1815: Napoleon Bonaparte rules France, with an interruption from 1812 until 1815.

1814–1824: King Louis XVIII rules France.

1914–1918: France fights in World War I.

1939–1945: France fights in World War II.

JUNE 6, 1944: The United States and Britain fight against German troops in France on D-Day, a decisive battle in the war.

1958: France elects President Charles de Gaulle and creates the form of government that it still has today.

1993: France and other countries create the European Union. This is a group of European countries that work together.

2017: France elects Emmanuel Macron as president.

This takeover was part of the French Revolution. The revolution lasted more than 10 years. People fought for a more **democratic** government because they felt the king and queen had too much power and did not treat the people fairly.

In the early 1800s, France had a military leader named Napoleon Bonaparte. He led the country in many wars. After Napoleon's rule ended, France had different leaders. Some were kings, while others were presidents elected by citizens.

FRANCE IN THE WORLD WARS

In the 1900s, France fought in World War I and World War II. During World War II, Germany took over France. The United States and Britain **invaded** France to help France escape from German control. This invasion on June 6, 1944, is known as D-Day. It changed the war. The United States, Britain, and France defeated Germany a year later.

In 1958, France formed the government that it still has today. The country elected President Charles de Gaulle. Presidents can stay in office for two terms, or 10 years.

FACT

During World War II, Germany took control of France's government. French people who continued to fight the Germans were called the French Resistance.

CHAPTER THREE

EXPLORE FRANCE

France is a popular country for **tourists**. Paris is one of the top 10 most visited cities in the world. It has many sites to explore.

FACT

Tourists liked visiting the Notre Dame Cathedral in Paris. But in April 2019, a large fire damaged the beautiful building. Experts said it could take two decades to repair.

Visitors can get a beautiful view of the city from the top of the Eiffel Tower. There are more than 600 stairs to the second floor. The tower looks over the Seine River, which flows through Paris.

ROAD TO THE ARC DE TRIOMPHE

The Champs-Elysees is a famous street in Paris. It is known for its shopping and entertainment options. The street has many high-fashion clothing stores. It also has restaurants and movie theaters.

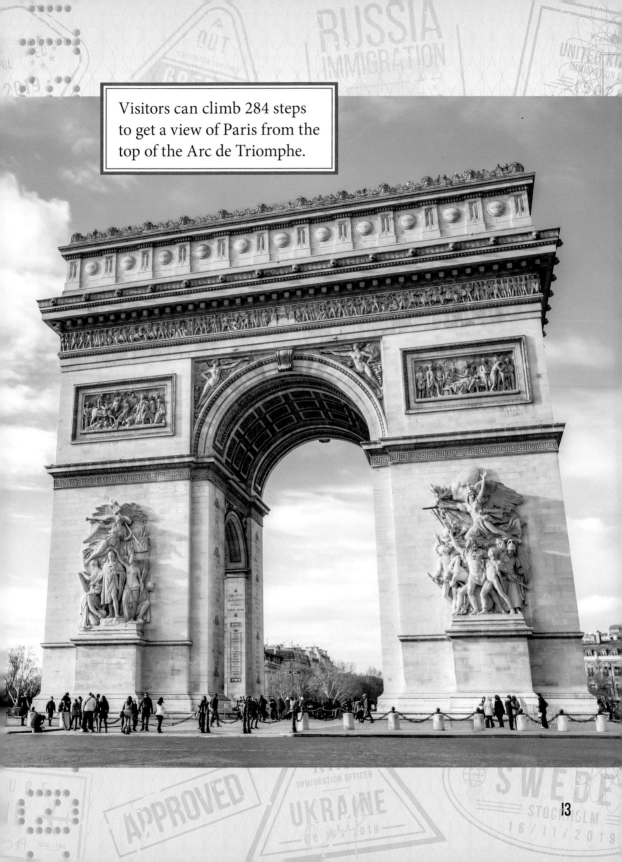

Visitors can climb 284 steps to get a view of Paris from the top of the Arc de Triomphe.

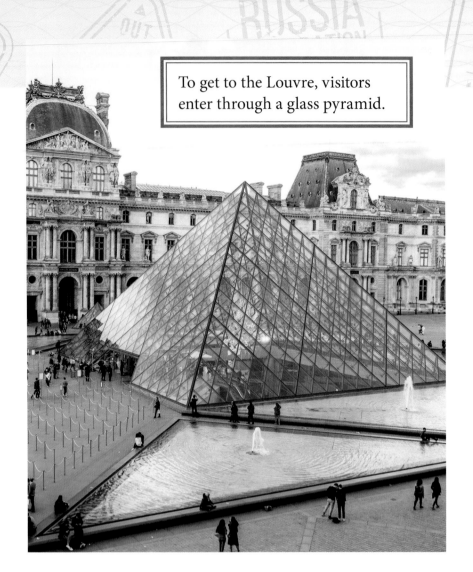

To get to the Louvre, visitors enter through a glass pyramid.

The Arc de Triomphe is the start of the Champs-Elysees. This large stone arch is at the center of a **roundabout** in the street. France's government started building the arch in 1806 to honor those who lost their lives at war.

MUSEUMS AND GARDENS

The Louvre, a popular art museum, also sits along the Seine River. More people visit it than any other art museum in the world. The Louvre houses many famous paintings, including the *Mona Lisa*. The museum has sculptures, drawings, and many other pieces of art too.

The Tuileries gardens are outside the Louvre. They have beautiful flowers and trees. The gardens also have statues and ponds.

Paris has many more gardens and parks. One of the largest parks is the Bois de Boulogne. This used to be a place where French kings hunted. Now it is a park for visitors. It has forest areas, lakes, and a waterfall.

FACT

The Bois de Boulogne is 2,100 acres (850 hectares). That is bigger than 1,000 soccer fields.

The most famous room in the Palace of Versailles is the Hall of Mirrors. It has 357 mirrors!

A GOLD PALACE

The Palace of Versailles is just outside Paris. Louis XVI and Marie Antoinette lived there. So did other French kings and queens. Now it is open to visitors. Versailles is known for its fancy art and decorations. It also has one of the largest gardens in the world. Workers at the palace plant more than 210,000 flowers a year!

People who like castles can visit the Loire Valley. This is outside the center of Paris. Tourists enjoy several castles and the beautiful countryside.

CITIES ON THE COAST

People love visiting beaches in France. Cities such as Marseille and Nice are on the Mediterranean Sea. This is in the south of France. Along with beaches, these **coastal** cities have museums, markets, and other places to visit.

SMALL TOWNS

Many people enjoy visiting small towns in France. One popular town is Giverny. About 500 people live there. Giverny was home to Claude Monet, a famous painter who lived in the early 1900s. Tourists can visit his house and see the gardens he painted.

CHAPTER FOUR

DAILY LIFE

Daily life in France is not so different from the United States. People go to school and work. The school year for French children is from September to June. They get July and August off for summer break. The school day starts at about 8:30 a.m. and ends at about 4:30 p.m. Students typically get a two-hour break for lunch. Some go home during that time.

THE SOUND OF BELLS

In cities and **rural** areas, people can listen to the beautiful chime of bells. Bells from old churches ring throughout the day. Some bells ring once every hour. People can listen to them while they relax outdoors at cafés or wait in line at theaters.

FACT

The French are known for their fashion. Paris Fashion Week is one of the biggest fashion shows in the world.

A bell tower juts high above the town of Saint-Tropez.

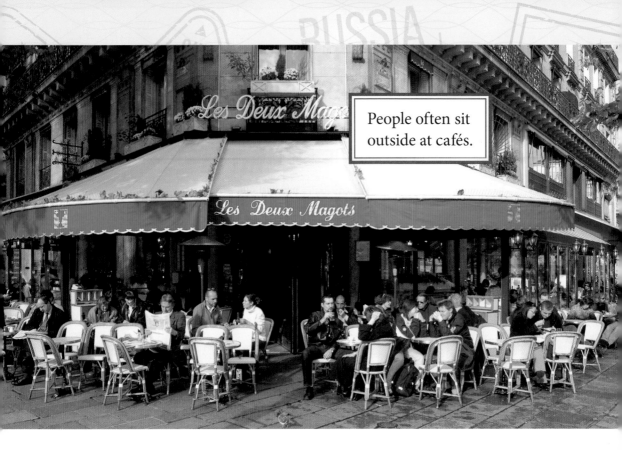

People often sit outside at cafés.

In these public spaces, **etiquette** is important. Many French people value respectful language and manners.

FRENCH MEALTIME

Food is important to French people. Their dinners often take a long time, since they have three courses instead of one. Dinners might include an appetizer, the main dish, and dessert. Meals are a time for friends and family to talk with each other. It is a French tradition to appreciate long mealtimes.

French food is famous around the world. Many cheeses come from France. French breads are common too. They bake long breads called baguettes and flaky pastries called croissants.

CROQUE MONSIEUR

With an adult's help, you can make French food at home. This sandwich is popular at French cafés. It is often served with bechamel sauce.

Sandwich Ingredients:
- bread (two slices)
- ham
- cheese
- butter

Bechamel Ingredients:
- 5 tablespoons butter
- ¼ cup all-purpose flour
- 1 quart milk
- 2 teaspoons salt
- ¼ teaspoon freshly grated nutmeg

Sandwich Directions:

1. Put ham and cheese between the two slices of bread.
2. Heat a frying pan on the stove over medium heat. Melt the butter in the pan.
3. Fry sandwich for three to four minutes on one side. Flip and fry other side.

Bechamel Directions:

1. Melt butter in a saucepan over medium heat.
2. Stir in flour. Let it cook until it is golden.
3. Turn heat to medium-high and whisk in milk.
4. Turn down heat to medium-low and let it sit for 10–20 minutes.
5. Add salt and nutmeg.
6. Spread sauce on sandwich.

CHAPTER FIVE

HOLIDAYS AND CELEBRATIONS

Some holidays are unique to France. One is Bastille Day. It is on July 14. During this holiday, the country honors the people who lost their lives during the French Revolution. There are parades and fireworks. People dance and eat together.

NATIONAL CELEBRATIONS

France observes Armistice Day on November 11. Other countries have this holiday too. The United States calls it Veterans Day. The holiday honors the soldiers who died in World War I. Some people wear black on this day. Parades show appreciation for the military.

France celebrates May Day on May 1. May Day recognizes people who work. Many businesses close.

Bastille Day is sometimes celebrated with red, white, and blue fireworks, the colors of the French flag.

The town of Colmar is famous for its Christmas markets.

On May Day, people give each other flowers called lilies of the valley. They relax with family.

RELIGIOUS HOLIDAYS

Christianity has a long history in France. About half of the French population still practices a form of Christianity called Catholicism. This means Christian holidays such as Christmas are widely celebrated in France. Many businesses and schools close for Christmas. People of other religions live in France too. A small number of French people practice Islam. They celebrate *la fête de la rupture*, or Eid al-Fitr. This period of three days follows a month spent fasting from sunrise to sunset. People enjoy big meals together during Eid al-Fitr.

FACT

May Day lilies are a tradition because of France's King Charles IX. He got these flowers as a gift on May 1, 1561. He liked them so much that he gave them to ladies of the court every year after that.

CHAPTER SIX

SPORTS AND RECREATION

French people enjoy many sports, and France even hosts famous sports events. One of the most famous is the Tour de France. It is a bicycle race across the country. Athletes from around the world participate. The race takes three weeks. It covers about 2,162 miles (3,470 kilometers). The race started in 1903. At that time most of the cyclists were French.

The Tour de France has grown into a worldwide event. People from faraway places such as Costa Rica and Australia participate. About 20 teams of nine riders race. Each year, people around the world watch it. Many see it on TV. Some travel to France to watch the race in person. There are parties across the country to celebrate.

Cyclists in the Tour de France ride through the Pyrenees Mountains.

The French Open is the only Grand Slam tournament played on clay.

TENNIS AND SOCCER

France also hosts the French Open. This is one of the world's largest professional tennis tournaments. Tennis players from around the world compete.

Soccer is the most popular sport in France. French people call the sport football. More than 2 million people play soccer in France. Many more watch it on TV. The France national team won the soccer World Cup in 2018.

ESCARGOT
· ·

Escargot is a traditional French game. It is the French word for snail, pronounced "ess-car-go." The game is like American hopscotch. You just need sidewalk chalk and a small group of people to play.

1. Use the chalk to draw a circle on the ground.
2. Draw a line coming out of the circle like a spiral wrapping around it.
3. Draw lines to divide the spiral into squares. Write a number on each square.
4. The first player hops in the spiral on one foot. The player hops on as many squares in a row as he or she can. The players cannot touch the lines. If the player makes it to the circle, he or she can pick any square. The player writes his or her name on it. Now no other players can hop on that square.
5. Players take turns. As more make it to the circle, more squares will have names on them.
6. The game is done when every square has a name on it. The winner is the person with the most squares.

Winter sports are popular in France too. People go skiing and snowboarding in the mountains. France is known for its sports, art, and more. Its food and fashion are famous. Many people visit the country. From castles to the Eiffel Tower, France is full of beautiful sites to see.

GLOSSARY

coastal (KOHST-uhl)
along the sea

culture (KULL-chur)
the way of life for a group of people

democratic (dem-uh-KRAT-ik)
having to do with a government system in which people vote on the way the country is led

etiquette (ET-uh-kit)
polite behavior in a particular society

governing (GUHV-urn-eeng)
ruling a country

immigrants (IM-uh-grints)
people who have come to another country to live there

invaded (in-VAY-ded)
entered a country and took control of it

monuments (MON-yuh-muhnts)
statues or buildings that are made to remind people of a person or event in history

roundabout (ROUND-uh-bout)
a circular intersection of streets that cars drive around

rural (RUR-uhl)
having to do with the countryside

tourists (TOOR-ists)
people who visit another country

READ MORE

Anastasio, Dina. *Where Is the Eiffel Tower?* New York: Penguin Random House, 2017.

Lanser, Amanda. *World War II by the Numbers*. North Mankato, MN: Capstone Press, 2016.

Pezzi, Bryan. *Eiffel Tower*. New York: Weigl, 2018.

INTERNET SITES

National Geographic Kids: France Facts
https://www.natgeokids.com/za/discover/geography
/countries/facts-about-france

Wonderopolis: How Tall Is the Eiffel Tower?
https://www.wonderopolis.org/wonder/how-tall-is-the-eiffel
-tower

Wonderopolis: What Is Bastille Day?
https://www.wonderopolis.org/wonder/what-is-bastille-day

INDEX

OTHER BOOKS IN THIS SERIES

YOUR PASSPORT TO CHINA
YOUR PASSPORT TO ECUADOR
YOUR PASSPORT TO EL SALVADOR
YOUR PASSPORT TO ETHIOPIA
YOUR PASSPORT TO IRAN
YOUR PASSPORT TO KENYA
YOUR PASSPORT TO PERU
YOUR PASSPORT TO RUSSIA
YOUR PASSPORT TO SPAIN